LAW AND INSTRUCTIONS

FOR TAKING THE

CENSUS

OF THE

STATE OF MICHIGAN,

IN THE YEAR 1874.

ISSUED BY THE SECRETARY OF STATE.

LANSING
W. S. GEORGE & CO., STATE PRINTERS AND BINDERS.
1874.

LAW AND INSTRUCTIONS

FOR TAKING THE

CENSUS

OF THE

STATE OF MICHIGAN

IN THE YEAR 1874.

ISSUED BY THE SECRETARY OF STATE.

LANSING
W. S. GEORGE & CO., STATE PRINTERS AND BINDERS.
1874.

EXTRACT

FROM THE

CONSTITUTION OF MICHIGAN.

ARTICLE IV.

SEC. 4. The Legislature shall provide by law for an enumeration of the inhabitants in the year eighteen hundred and fifty-four, and every ten years thereafter; and at the first session after each enumeration so made, and also at the first session after each enumeration by the authority of the United States, the Legislature shall re-arrange the Senate districts, and apportion anew the representatives, among the counties and districts, according to the number of inhabitants, exclusive of persons of Indian descent, who are not civilized, or are members of any tribe. Each apportionment, and the division into representative districts by any board of supervisors, shall remain unaltered until the return of another enumeration.

CENSUS LAW.

AN ACT to provide for taking the census and statistics of this State, approved February 9, 1853, as amended by Act 101, Session Laws of 1873.

Duty of supervisors and assessors to take census and statistics.

SECTION 1. *The People of the State of Michigan enact,* That it shall be the duty of the supervisor of each township and ward, and assessor of each assessment district, at the time of taking a list of the taxable property, or between the first Monday of April and third Monday of May, in the year one thousand eight hundred and fifty-four, and every ten years thereafter, to go to every dwelling-house in their respective township, ward or assessment district, and by personally inquiring of the head of every family, or some competent person, to ascertain and take an enumeration of all the inhabitants therein (except uncivilized Indians belonging to some tribe), in the following order, to wit: The names of all males of the age of twenty-one years and under forty-five (designating the married from the unmarried); the names of those of forty-five and under seventy-five; the names of those of seventy-five and under ninety; the names of those of ninety and under one hundred; and the names of those over one hundred; the number of females of the age of eighteen years and under forty (designating the married from the unmarried); the number of the age of forty and under seventy-five; the number of the age of seventy-five and over; the number of children under the age of five years; the number of the age of five and under ten (designating the males from the females); the number of males of the age of ten and under twenty-one, and the number of females of the age of ten and under eighteen; the number of colored persons; the number of blind; the number of deaf and dumb; and the number of insane persons and idiots; the number of marriages and the number of deaths the preceding year, as near as can be ascertained; and the occupation or profession of all males over twenty-one years of age.

Statistics to be collected.

SEC. 2. And it shall also be the duty of the supervisors and assessors of each city and township, at the time Idem. mentioned in the preceding section for taking the census of his township or ward, to ascertain and set down in a table prepared for that purpose the whole number of acres of taxable land; the whole number of acres of land owned by individuals and companies; the number of acres improved; the whole number of acres of land exempt from taxation, and for what cause, and its value; the number of acres sowed with wheat then on the ground; the number of acres and the number of bushels of corn harvested the preceding year; the number of acres harvested and the number of bushels of wheat raised the preceding year; the number of bushels of all other kinds of grain; the number of bushels of potatoes and the number of tons of hay the preceding year; the number of acres planted with the following varieties of trees: peach, pear, apple, plum, cherry; the number of acres planted with grape vines, with raspberry canes, strawberry plants, currant and gooseberry bushes; and the number of acres planted with melons and with garden vegetables, and the quantity of each of the following articles produced during each

Idem. of the two preceding years: apples, peaches, pears, plums, cherries, grapes, strawberries, currants, gooseberries, melons and garden vegetables, and the value thereof as nearly as it can be ascertained; the number of sheep, and the number of pounds of wool sheared the preceding year; and the number of sheep and the number of swine over six months old; and the number of pounds of pork marketed; the number of neat cattle (other than oxen and cows) one year old and over; the number of horses one year old and over; the number of mules; the number of work oxen and the number of milch cows; the number of pounds of butter and cheese made the preceding year; the number of pounds of sugar manufactured the present year; the number of pounds of fruit dried for market; the number of cans of fruit and vegetables canned for market during the preceding year; the number of cans of pickles manufactured for market; the number of pounds of peppermint oil manufactured the preceding year; the number of flouring mills, and the number of runs of stone in each; the number of barrels of flour made by each the preceding year; and the number of oil mills, and the number of gallons of oil made the preceding year; the number of breweries, and the number of barrels of beer made the preceding year; the number of distilleries, and the number of gallons of liquor made the preceding year; the number of gallons of wine made the preceding year; and the number of barrels of cider made the preceding year; and the number of barrels of fish caught the preceding year, and the amount of capital invested; the number of saw mills, and the number of feet of lumber sawed by each the preceding year and the amount of capital invested; the number and kind of all manufactories, the number of persons employed in each, the amount of capital invested and the value of the products for the past year, designating the number of said mills and factories operated by steam and the number by water power; the number of mines worked, the amount of capital invested, and the number of men employed, specifying the kind of mineral, the aggregate quantity in pounds, and its valuation at the place of mining; the amount of capital invested and the number of men employed; and the value of all the merchandise imported

Idem

the preceding year for the purpose of sale.

Duty of Secretary of State.

SEC. 3. The Secretary of State shall prepare proper blanks for taking the census and statistics, and shall transmit to the several county clerks of all the organized counties of the State a sufficient number for each township, ward, or assessment district in each county, on or before the first day of January, in the year of our Lord one thousand eight hundred and fifty-four, and every tenth year thereafter; and it shall be the duty of the county clerk to receive and retain the same in his office, and on or before the second Monday in April next thereafter, cause to be delivered to the supervisor of each township and ward, and assessor of each assessment district in the county, a sufficient number of said blanks for the supervisor or assessor to take the census of his township or ward, or assessment district (as the case may be), and to make a condensed statement thereof, as prescribed in the next succeeding section.

Census and statistics to be condensed by supervisor and assessor.

SEC. 4. It shall be the duty of each supervisor and assessor to condense the census and statistics of his township, ward, or assessment district, so as to show the aggregate number of each class, to write out distinctly the names of all males over the age of twenty-one years; and when so arranged he shall make duplicate copies, and personally deliver or forward the same to the county clerk of their respective counties, on or before the first day of July, next thereafter; and it shall be the duty of the county clerk to forthwith seal up one copy and send it by mail to the Secretary of State, and the other he shall file and carefully preserve in his office.

Duty of county clerk.

SEC. 5. If any supervisor or assessor shall be sick, or otherwise unable to perform, or omit to perform the duties required by this act, the township or city board shall immediately appoint a suitable person to do the duties of such supervisor or assessor, who shall take and subscribe the constitutional oath before entering upon the duties of his office.

When person to be appointed to do the duty of supervisor or assessor.

SEC. 6. Any supervisor or assessor neglecting or refusing, without good cause shown, to perform all the duties prescribed in this act, shall forfeit the sum of one hundred dollars, to be recovered by an action of debt, in the name of the people of the State of Michigan, for the use of the county where such failure occurred.

Penalty for neglect of duty.

Prosecuting attorney to sue for forfeitures.

SEC. 7. It shall be the duty of the county, township, or city clerk (as the case may be), to notify the prosecuting attorney of the county of any forfeiture under this act, who shall immediately commence a suit for the recovery thereof, and prosecute the same to a final termination.

Compensation of supervisors and assessors.

SEC. 8. The supervisor of each township and ward, and the assessor, of each assessment district, shall be allowed, in addition to the sum allowed by law for taking the assessment of his township, ward, or assessment district, two dollars for every one hundred persons by him returned, if the number shall exceed one thousand and five hundred; and two dollars and fifty cents per hundred for any number less; and ten cents per mile for conveying the returns to the county clerk's office, which shall be in full for all services performed under the provisions of this act; and the sum due each supervisor and assessor for services, shall be calculated at the rate aforesaid by the county clerk to which the proper returns are made, and his certificate of the amount due shall be paid by the treasurer of said county:

Proviso.

Provided, That before a supervisor or assessor shall be entitled to receive any compensation, he shall attach a certificate to each copy of said returns, signed by him, in the following form, to wit: "I do hereby certify that the census and statistics set forth in the schedule hereunto annexed, has been consolidated and arranged from enumeration and statistical lists, made by actual inquiry at the dwelling, or personal inquiry of the head of every family, or of a competent person acquainted with the facts, by myself, in the township of ——— ———, or ward number ———, in the city of ————, or assessment district in the city of ——— (as the case may be), and that the said schedule has been made in every repect in conformity with the act for taking the census and statistics for the year eighteen hundred and fifty-four, and every tenth year thereafter, and the amendments thereto, and is correct and true, according to the best of my knowledge and belief." Form of certificate to returns.

SEC. 9. The Secretary of State shall condense, in a tabular form, the census and statistical returns made to him, and, as soon as may be, cause three thousand copies to be published in pamphlet form, and transmit four copies to each organized township in Report of Secretary of State. Distribution thereof.

the State, one for the use of the supervisor, one for the use of the township clerk, and two to be deposited in the township library; and twenty-five copies to the mayor of the city of Detroit, and ten copies to the mayor of any other city in the State, for the use of the several city libraries, and one copy to each of the members of the Legislature and its officers: *Provided*, That in counties having less than five thousand inhabitants, the supervisor in each town shall be entitled to three dollars for taking the census and statistics in his town extra.

Proviso.

Common council of Detroit to appoint marshals.

SEC. 10. In the city of Detroit the common council shall appoint a person in each ward to discharge the duties required by this act to be performed by the supervisor of each township or ward: *Provided*, There is no assessor elected in said wards.

Proviso.

Columns to be footed.

SEC. 11. It shall be the duty of the persons required in this act to take said census, to have the several columns of figures footed, and the aggregate amount put down.

Governor to appoint marshals in certain cases.

SEC. 12. That the Governor appoint marshals to take the census in the unorganized territory not otherwise provided in this act, who shall receive such compensation as the board of supervisors of theorganized county to which such unorganized territory is attached for judicial purposes shall allow.

This act shall take effect immediately.

INSTRUCTIONS.

TO COUNTY CLERKS.

You will receive by express a supply of blanks, and pamphlet law and instructions for taking the census and statistics of the State for 1874.

The blanks comprise five printed schedules, and a quantity of ruled paper.

The schedules numbered 1, 2, 3, 4, are for the original work of *taking down* the information required to be obtained.

The other schedule and ruled paper are for the copies of *condensed statement of aggregates*, and names and occupations of males over twenty-one years of age, which enumerators are required to make, in duplicate, and personally deposit with, or forward to the clerk of their respective counties on or before the first day of July; one of which you are forthwith to seal up and send to the Secretary of State.

After the spring election, and on or before the second Monday in April, you will, as required by law, cause to be delivered to the Supervisor of each township and ward and assessor of each assessment district in the county, and in the city of Detroit to the persons appointed in accordance with law, by the common council, to take the census and statistics in wards where there is no assessor, a sufficient number of said blanks on which to take and return the census and statistics of his township, ward, assessment district or territory assigned him, and one copy of the pamphlet law and instructions to each.

In making the distribution of the schedules YOU WILL OBSERVE THE FOLLOWING:

The calculation for the number of each of the schedules numbered 1, 2, 3, 4, necessary to be printed, is based on an assumed population of one million five hundred thousand, and the number of sheets which it took to take the census and statistics for one thousand inhabitants in 1864.

Calculating by the number used in 1864, it is found that:

1 sheet of SCHEDULE 1 is sufficient for a population of 318.

1 sheet of SCHEDULE 2 is sufficient for a population of 400.

1 sheet of SCHEDULE 3 is sufficient for a population of 400.

And that of SCHEDULE 4 BUT 1 *sheet will be required by any enumerator*, except in rare cases in cities where manufacturing establishments are very numerous.

Of the SCHEDULE FOR THE CONDENSED STATEMENT to you and the Secretary of State, *two copies to each enumerator will be sufficient*, and the RULED PAPER for names, etc., to accompany the condensed statement, you will distribute at the rate of *one sheet for a population of eight hundred*, or a district containing 240 voters. A reasonable surplus of all the schedules and of the pamphlets, has been printed; a part of which is sent to you, and the remainder kept at the office of the Secretary of State to supply any deficiency which may be discovered; but as the type is distributed and no more can be printed in proper time, YOU MUST BE SURE TO ESTIMATE THE BLANKS NECESSARY IN EACH CASE CLOSELY, or the supply will be exhausted.

Should you discover that from any cause there will not be enough of any of the blanks, make application without delay to the Secretary of State for the kind and quantity needed.

TO SUPERVISORS AND ASSESSORS,

AND OTHER ENUMERATORS.

(Supplemental to the notes on the Schedules.)

1. Enter the items in *all* the schedules as well as in the lists of names carefully, with good black ink, to save time in deciphering defaced pencil marks, and for the sake of accuracy.

2. Make the enumeration and take the statistics *by families*, numbering and designating them so as to *know* when you are done.

3. All PERSONS TEMPORARILY ABSENT from home on a journey or visit are to be counted in their own family, but children and youth absent from home for purposes of education, on the first of May, and subsequently during the time of taking the enumeration, will be counted in the family where they are then living. Sailors, fishermen, railroad men, expressmen, etc., if they have a home and family in any particular place, will be counted with such family, and not where they may be temporarily, if away from home. *Care must be exercised lest the classes of persons referred to in this paragraph be counted more than once.*

4. Each page of the original schedules should be numbered *in order as filled, and when filled*, in the blank prepared for that pur pose, at the upper left-hand corner, numbering the first page of the first sheet PAGE 1; the first page of the second sheet PAGE 3, and so on. Exercise the utmost care to preserve your schedules, when filled, from loss or damage. Always carry the pamplet law and instructions.

5. Fill both sides of the schedules and be careful not to lose or spoil the blanks or *the supply printed may be exhausted.*

6. Enumerate DIVORCED PERSONS, as to social condition, with "widowers" and "widows"; those merely separated but not divorced, with the "married."

7. Designate the "PROFESSION, OCCUPATION OR TRADE" *closely*, as: "Stone Mason," "Brick Mason," "Clerk in Store," "Bank Clerk," "Retired Merchant," "Carpenter and Joiner," "Carpenter," "Cabinet Maker," "Shoemaker," "Huckster," "Dry Goods Merchant," "Coal Dealer," "Grocer," "Apprentice to Carpenter," "Works in Paper Mill," "Farmer," "Farm Laborer," "Miner," "R. R. Engineer," "Brakeman," "Hatter," "Hat and Cap Dealer," "Circuit Judge," "Probate Judge,"

(Judges will be understood to be lawyers, *the occupation of other officials should be stated*), "Fire Insurance Agent," "Life Insurance Agent," etc.

Reserve the term *manufacturer* for proprietors of large establishments, giving always the *branch* of manufacturing.

Distinguish between farmers and farm laborers.

Call no man agent, artist, professor, speculator, etc., without further explanation.

If a man works in (or for) a factory, state the fact, naming the kind of factory.

8. Report none BLIND who are not totally so, and only those INSANE of whose insanity there is no question.

Call none "DEAF AND DUMB" who are merely deaf and not dumb, or dumb and not deaf. Only such persons as can *neither hear nor speak* are meant.

The fact of IDIOCY can generally be best determined by the public opinion of the neighborhood.

9. As to MARRIAGES AND DEATHS, care should be taken to have it understood that the period covered by the inquiry is from the 1st of January, 1873, to the 31st of December, 1873.

10. The amounts of the various PRODUCTS will be *estimated*, where no exact account is kept, *from the best information which can be obtained from the proprietor or manager.*

11. By "IMPROVED LAND" is meant *cleared land*, whether used for grazing, grass, or tillage, or lying idle.

12. On all the Schedules where values are stated, *omit fractions of a dollar*, or cents.

13. Where a MANUFACTURING ESTABLISHMENT carries on more than one kind of business, each kind should be taken separately, *as to the kind of manufactures and their value.*

14. With MINES include QUARRIES, designating them properly as to the products. The reduction or manufacture of the products of mines, or quarries, whether connected with mines, or quarries, or otherwise, will be classed as manufacturing, and the works or mills for such purposes included under the head "Manufactories of all Kinds."

15. After condensing and making your DUPLICATE COPIES OF AGGREGATES AND NAMES AND OCCUPATIONS for delivering to the county clerks, on or before the 1st day of July, one copy of which he is to forward forthwith to the Secretary of State, *roll up the original* *blanks on which you have taken the enumeration and statistics, and forward them by mail or express to the Secretary of State.* BY SO DOING YOU WILL SAVE A GREAT DEAL OF CORRESPONDENCE WHEN THE CONDENSATION FOR PUBLICATION IS GOING ON IN THE OFFICE OF THE SECRETARY OF STATE. Errors will always creep in, in copying, etc., and *it is very important that the originals be at hand to refer to when the accuracy of any particular item seems improbable.**

16. By the preparation of the schedule on which to copy the condensed statements, which you are to deposit with the county clerk, A GREAT SAVING OF LABOR TO ENUMERATORS over the method heretofore in use, has been projected, and it is hoped by the Department of State that you will show your appreciation of its efforts to so simplify and reduce your work, under the law, as to render as far as possible the compensation allowed you, commensurate with your labor, by taking pains to *make the statistics of this census as perfect as possible,* and the best of the series.

* If, at the time of condensing, you find errors in the Schedules and correct them, change the incorrect marks in the original Schedule immediately, to save subsequent annoyance.

www.ingramcontent.com/pod-product-compliance
Lightning Source LLC
LaVergne TN
LVHW011144110826
845150LV00008B/2500
* 9 7 8 1 4 1 8 1 9 2 8 2 2 *